This book is dedicated to the Late Great

Dr. Maya Angelou.

She is the inspiration behind my writing poetry after reading
I KNOW WHY THE CAGED BIRD SINGS and hearing
her performing Spoken Word poetry on the television.

Praise for LaQueisha Malone

"Whoa! Whoa! Whoa! That was deep and mind blowing. The cover [Cell of the Mind] sets the mood for what is to follow, broken and powerful imagery portray the message *once was lost* and *now I'm found*...I felt the emotion that was released and awaited the evolution to follow. I loved the love of life that was pouring off of the page...real raw emotion...."
—Josie Just Josie, *Fashion Blogger*

"I love this [Cell of the Mind] compilation of shorts...LaQueisha Malone's poems are personal, yet addictive....It will both captivate you, and educate you..."
—Patron Gold, Author of *Cut Throat 1 & 2*

"[A Walk In My Shoes] Meaningful and soulful..."
—Pamela Wright, Author of *A Second Chance at Love*

"This book [A Walk In My Shoes] puts you in the heart of the Author and everyday life experiences and expectancy of the joys and sorrows of the word (LOVE!) ..."

—Sunshine Tatum, *Satisfied Reader*

A Walk In My Shoes

LaQueisha Malone

STRAWBERRY PUBLICATIONS
RISON, AR

STRAWBERRY PUBLICATIONS, LLC
PO BOX 895
RISON, AR 71665

Published by Strawberry Publications
ISBN 13: 978-0-6922-4354-1
ISBN 10: 0692243542
LCCN: 2014914796

Cover Design | Dynasty CoverMe
Author Photo | JT Studios
Author's Make-Up on Front Cover | Essence Wells
Author's Make-Up on Back Cover | Flowing Hands

For information regarding special discounts for bulk purchases, please contact Strawberry Publications at www.strawberrypublications.com

Printed in the United States of America

RE-RELEASE OF A NEW PAIR
OF SHOES STEP IN MINE

A Walk
IN MY Shoes

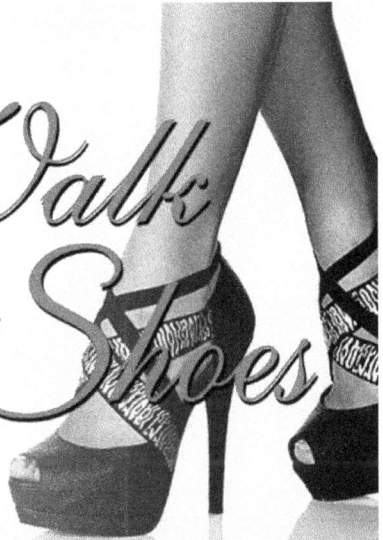

LAQUEISHA
MALONE

TRIP DOWN
MEMORY LANE
A POETIC MUSING

ACKNOWLEDGEMENTS

First, I have to thank God for bestowing this beautiful gift upon me. Thank you to my baby girl, Diovion, for giving me the mojo I need to be the best me I can be. You're the reason I push so hard. Mommy loves you.

To my mother and father, Pernella Brandon and Terry Malone, I love you guys for always being there for me. I hope you guys are happy with my achievements. Thank you guys for your unconditional love and support. A special thanks to my sisters, cousins, aunts, uncles, and close friends.

Thank you to Pamela Wright, the first author published under my book publishing company, STRAWBERRY PUBLICATIONS. You're such a great motivator. Thank you for believing in me. I will not let you down. You will always get the best of me in this business and with our friendship.

Thank you Shani Greene-Dowdell, author of *Secrets of a Kept Woman 1 and 2,* for being there in the beginning of my writing. You have helped and taught me a lot. You are my Shero.

Thanks to my family, friends, and enemies. You guys have made this possible. A special thanks to my cover designer Dynasty CoverMe for providing me with such a beautiful cover. I know I probably give you a hard time, but I love your work.

Marquette Williams, thank you. Your support was not only in words, but your actions and contributions allowed me to be in

"Aww" at your belief in me. And for that I will never let you or my family down.

Phyllis Williams, thank you for your friendship and for believing in me. You can always count on me.

Last, but not least, thank you to all the BlogTalkRadio Shows, Online Magazines, Internet Radio Shows, Blogs, Event Host, Readers, Bookstores, and Reviewers for making this book a success. Among those include The1Essence Radio Show, KnowUrEnemy BlogTalkRadio Show, Urban Grapevine Magazine, Black Stone Bookstore, and Fashion Blogger Josie Just Josie.

❧ Table of Content ❧

Thoughtless

". . .Blown away in the wind
Twirling in circles in the world it's in.
Bond with chains and shackles
Wanting to be free.
Face to the ground down on my knees

. . .Set me free I beg of thee.
I ignore my thoughts as they wonder away.
Flowing straight to the heart like a dart. . .
Oh! On this rainy day."

I'm Sorry

You said you were different, and to think,

I believed you.

I had to be blind and out of my mind to play this fool.

Break up and make up is the name of the game.

"I'm sorry, Baby. I'll never do it again believe me I've changed. I'll prove it to you if you give me a chance. You just can't give up on us now, you just can't. Not after all we've been through, smooth valleys and hard times. If you say it don't matter you'll be lying. Think about it, Baby, the ups, the downs. What about the love we shared does it mean anything right now?"

"I'm sorry, Honey. I've been holding on too long. You know as well as I know what you did was wrong. If the good outweigh the bad, we just might make it, but what you did I just can't seem to shake it. Don't get me wrong we can always be friends. You put me through too much, where do I begin? Tell me, if the shoe was on the other foot, and you were stepping in mine, what would you do? Where would you go? How would you feel in due time?"

Sweet Melody

*S*ome things are not always

what they appear to be.

Your thoughts lead you as far as the eyes can see.

*O*ne minute it's all Humpty-Dumpty glory.

The next it's all Dumpty- Humpty boring.

Sit down here and let me tell you a short story.

A favorite song only you two can share.

A song defining the love to show that you care.

*B*ut you've turned down a long bumpy road.

I guess that song of love you no longer hold.

*W*ait!! The song is playing,

and there are weeping eyes.

All you think about is what happened and why?

A Total Lie

He would tell me how I could change him.
I knew right then the chances was slim.

He said he's addicted like I am a drug,
but he never knew what it meant to give a hug.

I never could show it
'cause he was never around.
I knew what was going on,
him creeping and sleeping nowhere to be found.

It hurt me deep inside
'cause I thought he loved me.
Guess I played the fool I was blind I couldn't see.

I know everybody plays a fool sometimes.
Guess this turn was mine.

So, there I was all alone.
Left in the rain all night long.

I felt cold with no friends to understand

what I was going through, to lend a helping hand.

I was faithful, never untrue.

Nobody could see the pain I was going through.

I hope you know how I feel.

My love for you could've been real.

Just This One Time

This rivalry started between this one dude.
Had us arguing and fighting in that mood.
The very first argument we ever had
lasted a long time over what somebody said.

Hours have passed, and I've heard a lot.
So, now I see all this must stop.
When I build up the courage
I'll tell him to come.
I can't even face him to say,
"I'm sorry for what I've done."

There's this one sentence he said
that hurt me deeply.
A total lie.
A total lie completely.

Please forgive me for what I've done;
'cause I never want to lose you.
I want to know can we start brand new."

I Miss You

I'm missing you
and that's the hardest thing for me to do.

I miss you
telling me all the things I want to hear.
I miss you
pulling me close to you holding me so dear.

I miss you
gazing into my eyes.
I miss you
giving me that mysterious look and I wonder why.

I miss you
why can't I be where you are?
I miss you
I can't stand to be away from you this far.

I miss you
I want to look into your eyes.
I miss you
is there a knot we both can tie?

I miss you
the pain is hurting and it's for real.
I miss you
and the times we laid back and chill.

I miss you,
falling asleep in each other's arms.
I miss you,
cuddling together keeping each other warm.

I'm Sorry Baby

To let you know how sorry I am
words could not express.
Actions could never show,
but I'll do my best.

I put myself in your shoes
and I understand your pain.
I tried to get even
and I only cause shame.
For all the pain I felt
and loneliness inside.
I tried to cover it up and use a disguise.

I should have known better
than to play this game.
I let the rage of jealousy and envy
take over my name.
I'm truly sorry and God is my witness.
I let my vital take over and quit listening.

If you forgive me I promise
jealousy and envy I'll never know.
I love you and I never want you to go.
If you don't forgive me I'll understand.
You'll always be in my heart as that great man.

No Matter

We've made up, and put the past behind.
He even blew a kiss, now that blew my mind.
I'm loving it 'cause he's no longer mad.
Starting brand new forgetting about the past.
'Cause of hear-say my baby & I were into it.
It'll never happen again no matter who influence it.

Today I heard this song that
brought tears to my eyes.
Talking about the distance
between us that made me realize,
no matter what goes on stick by your man.
'Cause when you're down he's bound
to hold your hand and understand.

Rest In Peace

While you were here everything was cool.
Now you're gone I don't know what to do.
We've had good and bad times,
but in the end they always seem to work out fine.

From the moment I heard I felt empty and soar.
I cried and cried 'till I couldn't cry no more.
When I walked down the aisle
from my eyes drop some tears.
I looked at your peaceful face
telling me to have no fear.

You were gone to heaven my heart is at ease.
To my dear friend Rest In Peace.

In Love

When you're in love
it's not something you take for granted.
It's something you cherish, share, and feel.
Deep in your heart
you'll know if the feeling is real.
True love is also hard to define,
but as it slowly approaches you'll get a sign.

Some people ask,
"What is love? Is it steady?"
Then they look around and say
they're not ready.
You don't have to be ready for love.
Just as long as you know
what your heart is thinking of.

And You're Not There

I don't feel pain, just a little ache.

I feel lonely, by myself day after day.

I want to look at you.

Stare into your eyes.

Hear what you have to say

and question your alibi.

*Y*our testimony withholds no evidence.

It's almost irrelevant.

To sit here and say, "I'm cool,

my heads on straight,"

Would be a lie 'cause I'm losing it every day.

I'm hallucinating and calling out names.

Seeing bodies with your face.

Letting Go

Sometimes in life there are things to choose.

Even if it means the one you love you lose.

Sometimes it's a lesson you need to know.

That to pass the test the ones you love you let go.

It's not easy to do, losing the one you love.

Precisely over stupid stuff.

The pain you hate to show.

For the loved one you had to let go.

"Loving you was the best thing

ever happen to me.

You taught me a lot, and made me believe."

This may sound crazy, yes I know,

the one I loved I had to let go.

Sometimes in life there are

sacrifices with no guarantees.

Then you say to yourself, "Why me?"

But there are some things

you have to let show.

Just like love, you have to let go.

Why?

"Why does it have to be?
Why does it have to happen to me?"
That's what you'll say when some goes wrong.
You look as if you don't
but you know what's going on.

You may not understand.
You may not want to.
I know what you're thinking,
"Why? What can I do?"

I know how you feel.
Things like this happen to me.
So, I find myself saying
why does it have to be?
Believe me you're not alone.
And your thoughts won't let you go wrong.

Lonely Days

The only hard burden I have is that,

I have no one.

The past six months have been agonizing

the days are slow the come.

I'm so aggravated with every passing minute.

That I dwell on my past for a familiar feeling.

My days are dreadful,

and my nights are so very long.

Yet, and still, I thank God

for every day He help me carry on.

I Love You As A Friend

Every time I tell you I love you
don't mean let's get married.
I just like you as a friend
and you make me happy.
I feel you shy away from me
when I say those words.
I'm not ready to go there yet.
I'm not over the hurt.

I don't say it often
because it's not affection.
Before I do I have to gather feelings
I haven't yet collected.
You used to say it to me sometimes
and it felt so good.
If I ever thought
no one else loved me; you would.
I tried not to take for granted;
the times we shared.

*W*e had gotten so close,

then all of a sudden it just wasn't there.

I understand so I don't push the issue.

I just hope you feel that friendship I do.

I'll wait until you feel the same.

Just know that there's someone

who cares about you deeply

and you know her name.

Only Love

Devoting his time all to me.
Understanding and listening
making my life feel so complete.
I never appreciated
when he tried to get close.
Pushed him away
when I needed him the most.

He could see right through me.
What I feel, what I need.
When I told him to leave
I really meant stay.
He didn't understand that part.
So, he went away.

Staying awake all night long.
Day and night waiting by the phone.
It's because of love
that makes you wait.
It's because of love that'll make you stay.

Just the Way I Feel

Sometimes I think that things are unfair.
Sometimes I feel as if people don't care.
Some people wonder,
"Why do you always walk away?"
I say, "It's because you never make me stay."
I'll fill you in, if you want to know,
and if not just let me go.

How can I let you know,
when you watch me as I'm leaving,
while all of this on the inside
is heavily bleeding?
Maybe I need a shoulder just to cry,
or maybe a deep look in the eye.

When I begin to tell you what's on my mind
my feelings get in the way,
and I can't do it, not this time.
When I start to run,
after I've gotten so near,
you grab my arm and tell me to come here.

I begin to tell you, but I hesitate.
All of this on the inside
is trying to escape.

You grabbed my hand,
and looked in my eyes,
laid me on your shoulder
to comfort me as I cry.
You said, "I'll be here until the end."
You said, "I'll be there when you need a friend."

Nothing To Lose

A smile, to hide the pain.
Everything I've lost I'm trying to gain.
It's hard, trying to maintain,
when I have nothing to lose,
but everything to gain.

All that has been taken from me
I want it back.
I've been beaten up
and brutally attacked.

HELP!! HELP!!
It's hurting on the inside.
My tears are falling
as I close my eyes.

Please, take my hand
and be my guide.
Lead me through this,
so I can live my life.

I know if I stay I'll slowly die.
Can't you see it just look in my eyes.

*W*hy does it hurt this way?
It's hard to keep a smile day after day?
If you could see in my eyes
you'll know how I feel inside.
Help me figure out what to do.
What is there to gain
when I have nothing to lose?

I'm Waiting On You

I know you've been hurt
more times than a few,
but I got to let you know
how much I care about you.

When you're hurting inside
I feel your pain.
I watch you go through this
and all I can do is help,
but it I can't change.

You need to know that
You'll always have me.
When the night is too thick
and that better thing you can't see.

Sometimes I tend to look at you seriously.
What I feel for you is very passionately.
Sometimes it's as though I read your eyes.
All I know is the way I feel is strong inside.

Have I waited for you all this times?
Don't tell me the thought
has never crossed your mind.
That this could be what
you've been longing for.
It'll be different than before.

The New Beginning

A new beginning is hard to cope.
With a little faith, and a little hope
you can do just about anything.
Acknowledge your goals,
accomplish your dreams.

You don't know which way to turn,
because there's a flame of fire that still burn.
You can't turn and walk
away from the past,
when you have worked
so hard on what you had.

A new beginning is a bumpy road.
You have hills to climb, plains to cross,
who knows where this road may go?

The Night's Young & I'm Getting Restless

As I sit upon my stool,
twirling around acting like a fool,
I can't seem to keep myself entertained
because a sad section of love remains.
This love has taken a different turn,
but his flame of fire still burns.
The more I think of him
the more I cry.

I tell myself, "He's coming back
and there'll be no more lonely nights."
Sometimes that's hard to believe,
but I know our love will succeed.

Now the sun is going down,
and the night is creeping around.
I lay in my bed
with thoughts of him in my head.
Because of the one I miss
my nights get young & I get restless.

Do You See What I See?

As the night comes over the sky
I've had another day to wonder why?
The night has left me all alone
wishing I had someone
to keep me safe from harm.

I go sit and build up a storm,
I don't have anyone
to cuddle and keep warm.
All I do is daydream
how my life should be.
Just look in my eyes
and you'll see what I see.

Life's A Trip

I've always been told,
"You're too good of a girl."
But I find it hard to believe.
If the phrase was so true
then somebody would be loving me.

Because I yearn for love,
maybe that's why it's so distant.
But through it all I remain persistent.
Chasing after a shadow
that doesn't even exist.
Life's a TRIP.

I Don't Understand

One minute they're all over you trying to holla.

The next they're all over someone else's collar.

They must not know about that three-way deal.

That's how you know what's on the real.

They're kissing and sucking up,

throwing things in your basement.

While on the phone with your friend

trying to find a replacement.

What's up with that? And why is it so fake?

Be real about it and get it done face to face.

What's the problem? Why the persistent lies?

C'mon now. I can read between the lines.

Don't play me like a fool.

I know what it is you do.

The Lost Garden

How hard is it to find
someone to love me for me?
Is it that hard I have to go
after what I want to get what I need?
I don't like it like this
'cause I'm the one that gets hurt.

Tangled up in mixed feelings
trying to sort them out makes it worse.
How often do I cry?
How often do I lie?
I wear a mask a lot
so I don't have to wipe my eyes.

Dream

How often do dreams come true?

What does a dream mean to you?

Are they clear as a blue filled sky on a summer day?

Do they fill the sky with a rainbow on a cloudy day?

Which dream will enrich your life?

How do you know if what you feel is right?

If my dream came true in this lifetime

can't I wish it over and over a thousand times?

If my dream came true can I relive it over and over again?

Or live with the memories dwelling within?

If this dream I dream is only a dream

how will I know what my dream mean?

Day -N- Night

Watching day turn into night,

. . .can't wait 'til I see the morning light.

The sun is rising as the rooster crows.

What waits, I do not know.

My goal is to find true love.

. . .Only if I knew what that true love was.

The Feeling Love

What was it? I did not know.

This mutual feeling I was afraid to show.

It was scary, this feeling I knew nothing about.

I got real scared, I had no doubt.

Now I know what that feeling was.

I'm no longer afraid of the feeling love.

Distant Lover

When we talk on the phone to one another
I release emotions I can't seem to cover.
I maintain my cool as I try
to avoid this feeling I feel for you.

I tell myself over and over
that this is as far as it's going to go.
Beyond that saying there's a feeling
I have a hard time trying just to show.

I can't help the fact that
I want you to be mine.
Hoping that one day we intertwine.
I continue to be your friend
cause that's what I'm supposed to be.
But I still dream of the day
you'll be loving me.

A Wait

What is love to you and how is it shown?
Did it change or has it grown?
Is your definition the same
or has it changed the game.

Don't think that we can't
cause we know how to play the field.
If it's there, is it for real.
The love I feel is strong for you
and that's the truth.

My definition of love,
I'm staring it in the eyes.
It hasn't changed, something's
grown between you and I.
My heart's been broken
just like yours has.

I guess I wanted you to fix
it and messed up what I had.
Whenever you're ready

for love don't hesitate.
I'll be right here waiting
for you to come my way.

True Love

How long should I wait?
How long shall I cry?
I truly couldn't tell you the real reason why.
The long lonely days, the long lonely nights,
they fill my head with things that aren't right.

Now it's all behind me
my man has come.
I'm very happy life has just begun.
I've started bran new very slow not to rush.
As for right now, it's only a crush.

As time is slowly ticking, it's just him and me.
Now I know I'll love him eternally.
From the moments we share,
putting smiles on my face.
I know our love can never be replaced.

How Do You Know?

How do you know how you really feel?
Because I can't tell if the feeling is real.

How do you know if something is there?
Only time will tell from each moment we share.

How do you know what comes next?
I don't know what to expect.

How do you know if he's being sincere?
I can't even tell when he's being secure.

Do You Ever Wonder?

Do you ever wonder

how you really feel?

Do you ever wonder

what's the real deal?

Do you ever wonder

how you can look into their eyes

and never see the trace of a lie?

Do you ever wonder

when things are ever going to change?

Do you ever wonder

why it's all the same?

Do you ever wonder

what's on their minds?

I wonder it all the time.

Fighting Blind

These things people say you do
maybe they do them and put the blame on you.

Everyone has certain friends
that are hard to explain.
They are in your face one minute
then go out and scandalize your name.

These types of people you don't consider friends.
They were never there in the beginning
and never will be in the end.

What Is This?

If it's there in your face
what would be your sign?
If you're staring it in the eyes
why be so blind?

If you hear it every day
why give a deaf ear?
If you feel it all the time
what do you push away to get near?

If you hold on to it
how close is too close?
If you let it go
you might need it the most.

If you love everlasting
why should it end?
If you thought endlessly
before it begin?

If it's always around

where's it at?

You'll miss it

if you turn your back.

A Fools Gold

A fool never sees the light.
They're blinded by love
that makes everything alright,
so they say and I've also heard.
How do feelings get that involved
over three simple but beautiful words?

Why does this always seem to happen to me?
I've played the fool more times than a few,
am I that blind I cannot see?
Sometimes I wonder do people know
how much it really hurt.
They keep trampling over your heart
and burying your face in the dirt.

Sometimes I want to get away,
but how do a fool find themselves?
Will my actions speak
for all the pain I felt?

*W*ill the pain

be something I'll regret?
I try to put the past behind.
It's truly something I want to forget.

*B*ut every time a feeling is right

my feelings don't amount.
All the nights I've cried
I can't even count.

Dealing With Pressure

Lately it seems as if we've fallen
down a ditch calling
for one another, but we're
wondering around in a dark space.
Instead of using our hearts
to find one another
we've always got something to say.

May and cry when I'm alone
smelling your clothes
wishing you were here to hold.

I know sometimes it seems
as if I don't care, but I really do.
It's not fun, at the same time,
missing and loving you.

When I think about what you mean to me,
"My Whole Word Is You."
I try to deal with the pressure
and not include you.

They have always
told me above all odds
when you look at the face
of your loved one,
you're looking at the face of God.

So Many Questions

There are so many questions I have to ask.

Will they go unanswered?

Or will information be lacked.

Do you even know why you're gone?

Why you left me alone?

Is it because of a better life that's not meant?

What's all that worth

if you have no one to share it with?

The good and bad times...trying to get ahead.

Having someone there to hold you in bed.

I would love to share life's journey with you,

but there's little I can do.

Being thousands of miles away

doesn't leave a lot open.

Sometimes I feel like

I'm dreaming and hoping.

Flameless

The way you touch me
only lets me know you're for real.
The way you treat me, not only
lets me know, but feel.
Don't change; continue loving me.
It lets me know I'm all you need.

Rose petals in the bathtub.
Candles all around.
That's from me to you to
show you how I feel right now.

If you were to cook a dinner by chance,
played some music and we dance,
that would be enough for me.
It lets me know instantly you love me.
It don't take much to
please a woman this tamed.
Just always keep a flicker in this furnace
in case one day it turns into flames.

How Can You Love?

How can you love
when there's no one there?
How can you love
with only you and no one else?

Trying to make it you struggle and strive.
Don't give up keep hope alive.
You say you're in love with
someone you gave your trust.

How can you love them?
You know they don't love you,
but you ignore it 'cause
you know it's true.

How can you love
when there's no one there?
How can you love all by yourself?

Why Run?

Why run when there's nowhere to hide,
from all the pain you feel inside?

Watching day turn into night
you know something is just not right.
When the long lonely nights
follow the long lonely days
there's no one there to
comfort you in that special way.

You go and talk to a friend,
but they don't have that hand to lend.
You try and try to solve them,
but don't nobody want

to hear your problems.
You try and hide from what remains,
but no matter what you do you feel the pain.

Why run when there's nowhere to hide,
from all the pain you feel inside?

Have You Ever?

Have you ever said those three beautiful words?

Have you even tried to fight

the deep feelings that hurt?

Have you ever been so blind?

Have you ever been treated so unkind?

Have you ever wanted to throw it all away?

Have you ever wondered

when will it find a new place to stay?

Have you ever thought of this day,

or you never thought it would happen?

Not this soon anyway.

You'll Never Miss
A Good Thing Until It's Gone

A relationship is built on trust.

Without it you can't survive.

No matter how long and hard

you struggle and strive

to keep it alive.

Honesty, you should have too.

If you be patient he'll

open up his heart to you.

Don't be blind and play a fool.

Let trust and honesty be the golden rule.

You'll never miss a good thing until it's gone.

Don't let something so right become so wrong.

Can This Be True?

Beauty is in the hands you hold.

When your love over flows

and your story unfolds

to see the secrets untold.

Could he hold the key to the love I need?

When it's just he and I for eternity.

If this boy is mine give me a sign.

With him I'll sacrifice; to him I'll give my life.

Love is in the air.

I can feel it everywhere,

and to prove I care I'll always be there.

If I could hold you, would you hold me to?

I'm young, sad, and blue.

What else can I do?

The way I feel when I see you,

I can't hold it inside, I can't keep my cool.

This feeling of love is in my eyes.

You don't have to worry I'll never lie.

I really do need you.

I need you in my life.

I try and tell you, but the words

don't come out right.

My love for you is all so real.

How can I put into words what I feel?

I Love My Man

You don't understand, but I love my man.

The only one who's there for me.

The only one who cares for me.

The only one who shares with me.

The one that stares at me.

You don't understand why I love my man.

He holds me when nights are cold.

He comforts me when the days are long.

When he's hurt, I feel his pain and it hurts my soul.

When I cry, he consoles me

making all right what has gone wrong.

You don't understand.

I want the world to know I love my man.

On Our Wedding Day

Here we are together in a place

surrounded with love.

Who knew you were the one

my heart was thinking of.

I love you.

You're all I need.

Yes, I do.

You're the only one for me.

We'll be forever together.

Together forever.

To love, honor, and treasure.

To add more memories,

and reminisce on this day.

As our love for one another gets stronger,

in a very special way.

The Beginning of A Lifetime

The years have passed
and we've had ups and downs,
but through it all
you seem to always be around.

I know there have been times
you've wanted to give up.
I thank you for being there
when I needed a gentle touch.

You never pressured me,
but always kept it real.
That's why I'm here today
loving you still.

I Love You

Every night I lay in my bed
with thoughts of you that fill my head.
I know that I have done wrong,
and you have done wrong too.
But I'm letting you know
right now that I love you.

I would like to start over,
and forget about the past.
Because deep in my heart
I know we can make it last.

At the break of dawn
out peaks the sun.
I let you know
you're my only one.

It's morning and it's time
for us to say good-bye.
As I say this word
a tear drops from my eyes.

It's something I hate to do,
but I got to let you know I love you.

If you want to know why I love you?
It's because of everything you do.
I'm letting you know that I love you,
and hope you feel the same way, too.

First Impression

When I first met you
I didn't know what to do.
Should I just stand there and stare,
or go elsewhere?

I didn't know what to do so,
I dazed into my own little world.
But to him I'm just a little girl.
As time went by we became friends.
In my mind I hoped it would never end.

Only time will tell how I really feel.
I won't understand it,
but it's got to be real.

We lost touch somewhere in time.
What I felt cannot be defined.

Someone/Best Friend

Best friends are people who care.
People who understand your feelings.
Someone there in time of need.
Someone who is always willing.

A helping hand to lend.
It's all in a Best Friend.

Someone to tell your secrets too.
A Best Friend to let you know what's wrong.
They're always there no matter what's going on.

They're always around;
especially when things start going down.
They are there beside you letting
you know they'll never leave.
But you'll never know unless you believe.

When you believe it'll never end.
All for the love of your Best Friend.

So Wrong . . . So Right

I think about you day and night.
How can something so wrong feel so right?

I have a man he's nothing like you.
You fill me up when I'm sad and blue.

You turn my world around
and make my dreams come true.
I don't think I'll ever
find another quiet like you.

I think about you day and night.
How can something so wrong feel so right?

You treat me like I'm your everything.
You make me feel like a Queen.

In you I've gained a lot of trust.
My love for you is out of this world.
I just can't get enough.

Reminisce

As I reminisce on what we had.

It makes me feel so bad.

The chemistry was there.

I could feel it everywhere.

You played me using that same old line

in which you persuaded me time after time.

The relationship ended.

We're no longer together.

I thought what we had would last forever.

We're back together; spending so much time.

It seems like everything is working out fine.

I thought I was your only girl.

You made me believe I meant the world.

I don't know if this is right.

This feeling I feel deep inside.

Be About It

I know I'm shy; I know I'm quiet.

I guess you've never seen this girl be about it.

I know I'm picky and a little bit rowdy.

Guess you've never seen this girl be about it.

I've said all I've got to say.

No need to doubt it.

You know I can be about it.

All Alone Put To the Test

Here come the lonely days and lonely nights
It feels so wrong it's just not right.

I thought you'd be here with all of my days.
I still love you forever and always.

You should know for this is true.
I love you and everything you do.

Please think of me all the time.
Let me be constantly on your mind.

I can't say much else, so I put it to rest.
Because my love for you has been put to the test.

My Father

When you guys split up, I cried.
Each and every day I wondered why.
It was cool at first. Not much stress.
Until you started to come pick us up less.

The phone calls you never return.
The pain and the heartache
continues to burn.
It hurt inside.
Every time you lied.

You're our father nothing less.
All those times we've shared were the best.

In our heads, those memories we store.
Sometimes I wondered if you cared anymore.

Before he married he was great.
Now it seems as if we don't know him,
but we will keep the faith.

At first he came all the time.

Lately it seems not to cross his mind.

We love our father true enough,

but just like him...we need love.

Thinking Of You

As I lay right here and now.
Thinking of you feeling a little down.
I let you walk out of my life.
Now you are no longer by my side.

Memories of the good times feel me up.
When I close my eyes, I reach out for your touch.
I grab your hand, and you grab mine.
As we slow dance back in time.

The song goes off.
I open my eyes.
Only to find you're not by my side.
So I hold my pillow tight and dream of you.
For now, that's all I can do.

The Words, "I Love You"

The words, "I love you,"
should be said with meaning.
Never misused or mistreated.

Misusing the words, "I love you."
Believe me you are bound
for what goes around comes around.

Because the words, "I love you,"
is something you shouldn't play with.
If you don't mean it don't say it.

If the words, "I love you," get treated like dirt.
You better believe you'll get your feelings hurt.

Could It Be

Do you love me as much as I love you?
Don't lie to me tell me the truth.

It's got to be love that makes you feel this way.
Because I really don't care about what people say.

I know I have in the past,
but I'm willing to make it last.

Can't you see the situation
that's tearing our love a part
is lack of communication.

It's All About You

I like being with you, and all the times we share.
Your love is way beyond compare.

I want to be with you my whole life long.
Because loving you is so right,
and I don't want to go wrong.

You put smiles upon my face.
In and out of this world
your love can never be replaced.

What you do to me and the things you say.
Touch my heart in a very special way.

The One I Give My Heart Too

You told me you loved me.
You told me you cared.
I believed everything you said
out of all the times we shared.

I thought what you said was true.
I felt the same way too.
The magic in your eyes
makes me realize
that everything I feel
has got to be real.

I guess my feelings deceived me.
Once again I feel so empty.

I gave you all of my love,
and all of my time.
You did me wrong because
love had me so blind.
I'll be a little more careful
about the things I do.

Especially towards

the one I give my heart too.

You and I

I will always be right by your side.
Morning, noon, and night.

*Wh*enever you're feeling
down no need to sigh.
Because forever and always
it will be you and I.

*Wh*en it seems as if times get tough.
You can call on me and tell me what's up.

*D*on't worry.
I'll never say good-bye.
You won't go through it alone
it will be you and I.

*T*ell me what's on your mind.
Don't be shy.
We'll work it out together just you and I.

Eternally

When I gaze into your eyes, I see love.

Nothing but the two of us.

Eternity, forever, and a day.

Loving you forever and always.

Giving you all my love.

Showing you what's on my mind.

Candlelight dinners and the finest wine.

A gift for you. A gift for me.

Can you believe it's our anniversary?

We've made it through the years,

loving each other forever,

knowing we'll always be together.

Make It Last

Holding you close keeping you warm.
We've made it through the tragic storm.

If anything is wrong, I'll make it better.
Me...myself; loving you forever.

Turning your world inside out.
Caressing you without a doubt.

Letting you know you're very special to me.
Very special indeed.

I'm not going to rush just so you know.
I just want to take it nice and slow.

Deeply Within

Come! Go with me.
To a place where people go.
One another they get to know.

It's nothing like sin.
It's lurking deeply within.

It's an exciting thing to know.
Never turning its back on you and grow.

It's nothing like sin.
It's lurking deeply within.

Full of responsibility no doubt.
Your personality is what I'm talking about.

Why I Love You

At night the last face I see.
I thank the Lord for
sending your love to me.
He sent you to me
to love you eternally.

When I was down,
like no other friend,
you were around.

To lift me up, and hold my hand.
Always there to understand.

What I'm going through,
and wanting to be down.
When my friends
were nowhere around.

In the morning I'm greeted with a kiss.
And also a well-cooked breakfast.

Call On Me

When you're feeling lost and afraid.

When you fear what people might say.

Call on me and I'll come running to you.

There's nothing in this world

for you I wouldn't do.

When you feel like

you're just about through.

Just remember, "It's all about you."

Call on me I swear I'll never let you down.

Because I'll always and forever be around.

A Memory

Thinking of you all day and all night.
It feels as if you're right by my side.
If you do exactly what I say.
You'll think of me too.
All night and all day.

Turn on your favorite song.
Go with me and play along.

Lay in your bed. Close your eyes.
Put me in your head and fantasize.
Think of us under stars and moonlight.
Anything that comes to mind will be just fine.

Whether we're over at your place,
or dancing face to face.
Whether it's a memory, so soft, real sweet.
It'll be perfect, really neat.

After a while you can feel a touch.
A touch of love that mean so much.

*D*on't get scared.

Your thoughts are taking control.

Using your mind body and soul.

When you awake, you'll want to do it again.

For you have found love deep within.

Holding On

Whenever life is getting tough hold on.
Don't let it get the best of you stay strong.
I'll be there when you need me.
Call on me and you will see.

Nothing in this world
is worth losing you.
Please don't go.
Say you'll stay with me too.
I'll hold on and stay strong.
Because your love carries me on.

You Make Me Feel

My stomach is filled with butterflies
when I'm with you.
That's why I don't need no one else but you.

The things you do, and the moments we share.
It lets me know just how much you care.

The only way to give it back to you
is by doing the same thing you do.

A candle lit dinner, and our favorite song.
You and me together all night long.

Sometimes the memories change our style.
You make me feel like I'm worth a while.

Happy Valentine's Day

I have been with you for a while now,
and I love having you around.

*N*o one can smile like you.
No one can touch me like you do.

I love you I must say.
I want to be with you forever and a day.

Get O-U-T

The secrets are hard to hide.
After all, out of your mouth came a lie.

Your down lows. Your creeps.
I'm sorry, but get o-u-t.

You're dong me wrong.
You know you ain't right.
Staying out late.
All day and all night.

I want to be right if loving you is wrong.
Because of my friends is why I'm holding on.

It gets me all choked up.
I'm no longer denying
how I stayed up all night crying.

Your smile and sometimes your eyes.
Catch me off guard. They catch me by surprise.

The way you hug me and hold my hand.

Is not enough to let me know you're my man.

Now your time is way past due.

You have to leave.

I have to get over you.

A Thin Line Between Love and Hate

There's a thin line between love and hate.
A thin line that can't be erased.

One night of passion can lead to a lifetime of pain.
Play your cards right; know the rules to the game.
Getting caught all up in your mix.
Once that heart has been broken
it's hard to get fixed.

Playing around with people's mind.
Will only get you hurt somewhere in time.
God's watching every move you make.
Each and every heart you break.

He's going to punish you for your false alibies.
From the heartaches and pain off your silly lies.
Your ways will catch up with you one day.
Change your life in a mysterious way.

There's a thin line between love and hate.

A thin line that can't be erased.

Just To Be Near

There's nothing in this world I wouldn't do.
Especially when it comes to getting next to you.
I want to be where you are, or at least near.
I'm not happy in this lonely place here.

My imagination goes far and wide.
But it's not enough to put love aside.
I don't understand how love takes control.
It takes over your mind body and soul.

Guess that's why love has no limit.
It goes on and on until your mind is out of it.
And once you're gone, it's head over heels.
Just that one picture is a thrill.

Starting today I'll do everything I can
to bring you home and make you my man.
I shut the door to the wrong you've done.
Anything for us to be as one.

When I'm With You

When I'm with you the sun shines my way.
My love for you gets stronger each and every day.

When I'm with you there's one thing on my mind.
How to make you happy,
and make you smile all the time?

And when I'm with you, you brighten up my day.
I don't know what you're doing
to make me feel this way.

When I'm with you and look into your eyes.
I see heaven, and I know I'll love you for all times.

When you're not here I'm sad and blue.
Then you come and say, "Baby, I love you."

My heart beats fast I don't know what to do.
I feel a thrush of fever when I'm with you.

If I Could I Would

*I*f I could hold you one more time.

It will be ever so gentle your inquiring mine.

*I*f I could take you and hold you real tight.

It would be with passion just one more time.

*I*f I could hear, "I love you."

It would just blow my mind.

If I could I would just one more time.

*I*f I could look into your eyes,

and see everything that's on your mind.

I would heal your pain

with comfort just one more time.

No One Can See

No one can see the joy in my eyes.
No one can see in-between the lines.

No one can see what I feel inside.
These feelings I know I can't deny.

A feeling so strong but sure.
I know our love will endure.

I Saw You

I can remember your smile.

Your laughter is very strong.

It stops all right from going wrong.

As long as I can remember,

you're always in my heart.

As long as it's there we'll never part.

Come share my world and become one with me.

There's no need to make-believe.

Happy Mother's Day

You gave me life.
You gave me all my hopes and dreams.
I love you Mama.
You mean the world to me.

Teaching me right from my wrong.
With the strength to carry on.
Helping me grow healthy and strong.

Protecting me from evil and harm.
When I need love, you're there with open arms.

No one could ever take your place.
I love you forever and always.

One Moment In Time

One moment in time
you'll think you've found destiny.
Then sometimes you'll say is love really made for me?

One moment in time you'll realize true love.
That you and I should be together.
A sign sent from God above.

One moment in time we'll be together.
Loving each other always and forever.

Happy Father's Day

Through thick and thin you've been by my side.

Like a constant friend that'll never die.

Through good and bad you're there all the way.

Today is set aside for you.

Enjoy your day.

Just the Little Things

You comfort me all through the night.

Until I see the morning light.

Your voice calms me down

when my mind is lost and nowhere to be found.

Your eyes lead me back home.

Giving me strength to go on.

Your hands give me a gentle touch.

It's just the little things that mean so much.

Be As One

How can you tell if the feeling is mutual?

It seems to me rather unusual.

But when it comes down to loving you,

there is nothing I wouldn't do.

Through misery, agony, and pain.

I will shield you from the unexpected rain.

It's just the little things that mean so much.

Through all of your hard times when they get rough.

Love

Can't explain what I feel.

This feeling inside.

Could you be the love of my life?

I can't always show it.

My feelings for you.

What you're feeling I'm feeling it to.

I know that we both may not understand.

All I know is I'm ready to put my heart in your hands.

The warmth in your eyes,

and the kindness in your heart.

I don't know what I'd do if we were to ever part.

Stay by my side for the rest of my life.

I can no longer deny what I feel inside.

Love's In Your Face

When you turn to your right and then your left
I'll be there; I'll never let you be by yourself.

I'll be there to listen.
I'm there all the time.
To help with what you're going through
and help ease your mind.

I'll lift you up and bring your troubles down.
Helping you realize the good thing you've found.

Our love will linger on.
You can't go wrong.

Digging On You

I'm digging on you.

I hope you're digging on me too.

I'm sitting here thinking

of how to make you mine.

I think you're cute, and yet so fine.

I'm digging on you.

I hope you're digging on me too.

Fool In Love

How can this be?
That you're not here with me?

It's hard to go on without you.
What is it I'm supposed to do?

I want you by my side.
I need you in my life.

I put you on top and above.
I guess I was just a fool in love?

I thought your love was for me.
I guess what we shared was just a fantasy?

I was denied and very much betrayed.
I can't believe you'd up and leave me this way.

How could you do this to me?
I thought I was your everything.

$\mathscr{I}$wanted to move on and leave you behind.

But I couldn't leave what I thought

was rightfully mine.

$\mathscr{I}$guess I couldn't have you for myself.

All this time there was someone else.

Creeping Around the Way

I saw you on the corner chilling with your friends.
I wasn't listening to mine because I was digging.
All that day you were on my mind.
When it came to my friends I had no time.
I bumped into you on the street.
And you act like you couldn't even speak.

I've been creeping around the way.
Coming by where you live almost every day.
Wishing you would notice me.
But never did I dream it would be you and me.

We were swinging to a slow jam.
It was time to make my move.
Because this time I'm not going to lose.
I got to tell you how I feel.
Why I creep around you way.
Peeping you almost every day.
Finally it's you and me.
This is how it's supposed to be.

*L*ast night I rode by your crib

And your boys were stepping up to me.

They quickly bagged down

because they know how you live and be.

How Could You Do It?

How could you do it?

Leave me all alone.

How could you do it?

Leave me at home.

I woke up this morning

to find you were not there.

I guess you never loved me.

I bet you never cared.

How could this have happened?

Is what I'm trying to say.

All this time you have done nothing but play.

I guess I have to move on.

I can't let you get to me.

I've got to stay strong.

How could you do it?

Leave me all alone.

How could you do it?

Leave me at home.

What Has It Come To?

What has it come to?
All of this.
Do you show me you love me
by the power of your fist?

All we've done is argue, fuss, and fight.
It wasn't like this in the beginning.
Now I know something is just not right.

A loving couple were we.
How could this be?

You say you're sorry,
but save the lies.
I can't go through with it.
Believe me I've tried.

Can You?

Can you tell me what I need to hear?
Do you need to whisper it softly in my ear?

If what you tell me is true,
then why are you ashamed?
I hesitate to fall for it
because I know it's all a game.

The things you're telling me
I've heard every line.
You play around to get me
and then lay me to the side.

You said you can give me the world.
I guess you'll get it.
I'm not a materialistic girl.

All you do is play with minds.
Trample over hearts because you think you fine.

My man is true

Doing the things you proclaim you can do.

Can't Go Through With It

I don't want to argue all the time.
I'd rather lose you than lose my mind.

*A*ll the time we fuss and fight.
You stay out late all day and all night.

I don't think I can take much more.
God knows I've tried.
If I tell you I'd like to stay here
Just know I've lied.

I can't keep going through this same routine.
I have to rid myself of you for my sanity.

Make Up Your Mind

You say you love me.
How do I know?
You don't even treat me good.
Maybe I should go.

How do I know if what you say is true?
How do I know if it's just some kind of excuse?

Every day you sing the same old song.
Something's just not right.
You're babbling on and on.

Do you believe in trying to make things work,
Or just assuming the worst.

I need to know if you're having doubts.
It's obvious to see
you don't know what love's about.

I want to make things work,
but I can't if you keep treating me like dirt.

If I am not what you want, or what you need
I know there is somebody out there
Who can love me for me?

Can't Play the Fool

Tell me why you lie?
I put all my trust in you.
There was no wrong you could do.

Yet I see you've hurt me once again.
I'm broken hearted.
I don't think it'll ever mend.

You have lied to me for the last time.
I'm serious I have made up my mind.

This relationship has got to end.
It takes a fool to lose twice and begin again.

As much as that is true.
I've already been that fool.

I've been there once before.
And I can't take it anymore.

The Things They Will Tell You

You told me you love me.
You told me you cared.
You told me you needed me,
and that you'll always be there.

When it comes down to responsibility,
taking care of what's yours,
you act like you don't know me anymore.
To believe you I must have been crazy.
You've been dodging me ever since
you found out I was having you baby.

We don't need you or your lies.
My baby doesn't need a father like you.
Sooner or later you have to wake and realize.
A part of you is inside of me.
Step up and take care of your responsibility.

You Call On Me

In times of trouble when things are going wrong
and you can't keep your head up and stand strong.
You can call on me.

Whenever you're down and
you need someone to talk to.
When your friends are not there
and you don't know what to do.
You can call on me.

When you feel like you want to move,
and you feel as if you want to stay.
I'll come and help your find your way.
You can call on me.

As you sit there looking out you window pane,
the hurt is hard to bare
and your tears are falling like rain.
It's hard to contemplate.
You want to move on, but you feel it's too late.
You can call on me.

In life things are not always going to go your way. But no matter what be careful of the road you take.

Where Were You?

I lie awake in the middle of the night
with my private thoughts.
The silence is so loud it attacks my heart.

I want you here to hold me.
My happiness only you can protect.
Don't let these nightmares manifest.

I roll over to that cold chill
that lay on your side of the bed.
As those 4 AM thoughts crowd my head.

~THE END~

Turn the page for a sample of
the upcoming release from
Pamela Wright of
Strawberry Publications.

Release date: November 1, 2014

A SECOND CHANCE AT LOVE
Series 1
A CHANCE ENCOUNTER

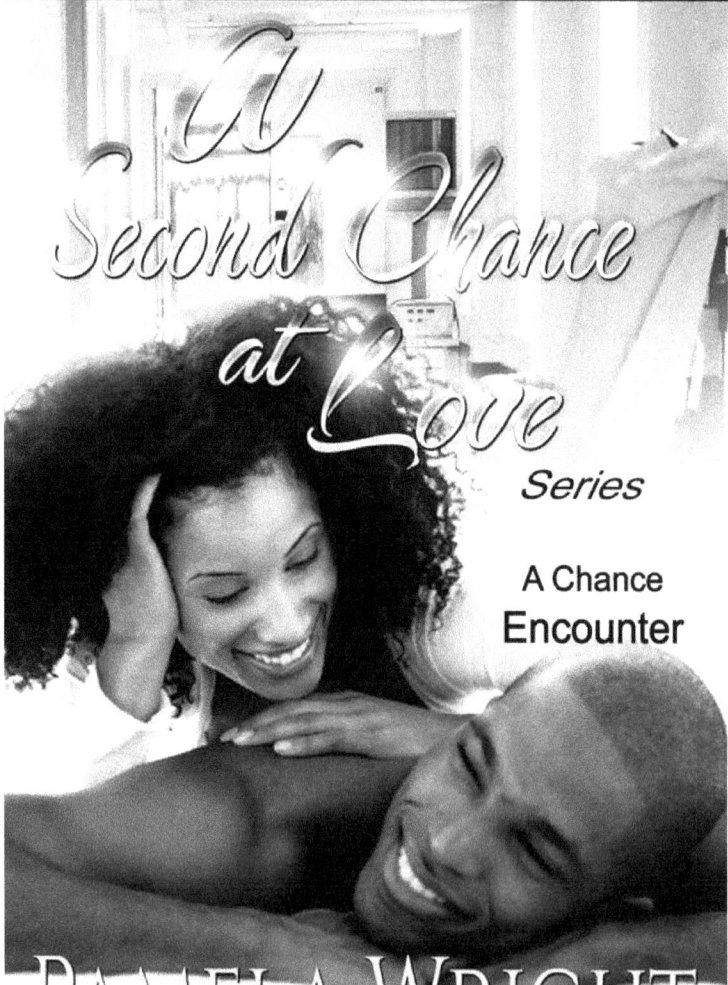

STRAWBERRY PUBLICATIONS PRESENTS

A Second Chance at Love

Series

A Chance Encounter

PAMELA WRIGHT

Chapter One

As Vanessa lay on the sofa, watching a home video of her tenth wedding anniversary, there came a knock at the door. *Not today,* she thought to herself. This was her moment of solitude. Her moment to do whatever she felt and no one was going to stand in the way. She turned the volume down on the television hoping the knocking would go away, but it grew louder. Agitated, she glanced over at the clock. For the past two months, her mother made it a point to come over every Sunday after church to check on her and the house.

"I know you're in there," Alice chimed while knocking with every word. Alice Pryor was a strong-willed woman, who knew how to get her way. She was not leaving until Vanessa opened the door.

Peeking over the sofa, Vanessa watched as he mother went frantically from one window to the next, pressing her face into the glass. Vanessa slouched back down into the cushion of the sofa. She loved her mother very much, but if there were ever a day she did not want to be bothered, today was that day.

"Open up!" Alice demanded.

Realizing her mother wasn't going to leave, she fixed her face, and took a deep breath before answering the door.

"Mom, come in," she said with a smile. "How long have you been out there?"

Her mother hurried passed, giving the house a quick glance. Studying her daughter's expression, Alice did not buy into her feigned innocence. "You're not fooling me. I know you heard me knocking."

"Mom, I was in the bathroom," Vanessa tried to explain, but from the squint of her mother's eye, she knew it was best to quit while she was ahead.

"You know you shouldn't lie to your mother." Alice exclaimed, then slowly walked to the den, and opened the curtains. The house was dark and smelled of last week. After grabbing a can of air freshener, she sprayed it into the air. She looked at Vanessa and was disgusted by what she saw. Her daughter looked like she hadn't bathe in days. Her once well-groomed, thick, beautiful hair now stood matted on Vanessa's head making her look like a beastly creature of the wild. Sleep coated her eyes, and her lids were puffy. It was the middle of the day, and Vanessa had on an over-size t-shirt and sweat pants belonging to her husband, Joe. Alice shook her head in shame.

"What, Mom?" Vanessa begged while brushing her hair back with one hand.

"I haven't said anything."

"No, you haven't spoken any words, but you've said plenty."

"You're in a mood today. Why?" Alice asked.

Oh here we go, Vanessa thought, watching her mother scan around the room. "I'm waiting on you," she said with a wide, condescending smile.

"Waiting on me for what?" Alice asked, placing her purse on the coffee table before sitting on the sofa.

"Aren't you going to say anything about the way the house looks?"

"What do you want me to say," Alice said, brushing crumbs from the sofa.

"Oh, I don't know. Why don't you tell me how messy the house is and that I need to clean up?" Vanessa said, kicking over a pile of newspapers that were in the middle of the floor as she joined her mother on the sofa.

"I don't have to tell you something you already know," her mother said reclining back against the sofa. "Why aren't you dressed?"

"For what?"

"I called yesterday. I told you I was taking you out for an early dinner today and you agreed."

While resting her head on the back of the sofa Vanessa closed her eyes. "Mom, I'm not in the mood for going out."

"You're never in the mood for doing anything. You look awful. When was the last time you changed clothes?"

"I change clothes every day. Are you saying that I stink?" Vanessa sat up defiantly.

"I'm not saying that. Why are you trying to pick a fight?"

Vanessa took a deep breath and exhaled. "Mom, I love you. I know you mean well, but—"

"What are these boxes doing here?" Alice interrupted.

"I decided to box up some of the kids' things and put them in storage."

"Can I help? I'm not doing anything," her mother said.

"I got it, Mom. I wasn't planning on doing it today."

"Since we're not going to go out for dinner, let's straighten up a little."

While picking the trash up from the table, Alice noticed a realtor's business card. She picked it up and turned toward Vanessa. "What's this?" she asked, continuing to clean up the mess.

"Oh, that's the card from Janice. She's the realtor who's selling my house."

"What?" Alice asked as she studied the card before turning her attention back to Vanessa.

"I told you last week I was putting the house up for sale."

"You told me you were thinking about putting the house up for sale. I didn't know you had already made the decision."

"Here we go!" Vanessa murmured as she stood, rolling her eyes to the ceiling.

"I know you don't want to hear this, but I'm going to say it anyway. You're making a big mistake by selling this place." She raised her hands as she looked around the room. "This is the house you and Joe made a home for your family. This is your dream home." Walking around, looking at the photos on the mantel, Alice smiled. "I remember when you and Joe found this house. You were so excited. The two of you were like a babies with new toys."

A smile crept over Vanessa's face. She remembered how much fun they'd had picking out the paint colors, choosing the window frames, and even tearing down the back porch and rebuilding it. A soft laugh escaped her lips. "Remember that barbeque when I tripped on the edge of the pool and fell in with the cake?"

"I remember that," Alice said with a giggle.

Vanessa picked up her wedding photo off the shelf. She gently ran her fingers across Joe's face before placing it back among the other photos. "There are memories of my family everywhere, and it's driving me crazy," she said, closing her eyes with tears rolling down her cheeks. Looking over at the kitchen table, she could see Joe reading the morning paper. With a glance out the window, she could see the kids riding their bikes and running through the sprinkler. The tears began to sting Vanessa's face and she dropped her head. Her mother touched her shoulder interrupting her trance. "I'm lost, Mom. I'm tired of living alone. I'm tired of being alone. I feel like I'm going insane."

"Baby, you're not going insane. You're grieving over a huge loss that would cripple most people. What you're feeling is normal."

"Nothing about my life is normal, Mom. Normal is having my family here with me. Normal is enjoying the life that I worked so hard for. Normal is celebrating holidays and birthdays with my family. Normal is growing old and gray with the man I love. Loving Joe for the rest of my life is not the problem; it's him not being able to love me back."

"You've lost a lot..."

"You've lost a lot! You've lost a lot!" she screamed, mocking her mother. "I'm so tired of everyone saying that. I know what I've lost. I'm not crazy."

"I know you're not crazy. I'm just saying, with everything you've lost, do you want to lose your house as well?"

"Mom, at this point it doesn't matter. In a couple of months, it will be three years since the accident, and I'm at a standstill. I'm looking forward to death."

"You don't mean that," her mother said sternly.

"Yes ma'am, I do. Don't you see mom? It's over for me."

"It's not over. I don't ever want to hear you talk like that. There's nothing that the God I serve can't fix, even a broken spirit." Looking at Vanessa, tears started to roll down her cheeks, and her heart started to break. She could see the agony that her baby girl was going through, and there was nothing she could do to ease the pain. Alice yearned for the times when Vanessa was happy and excited about life.

Vanessa walked over to the sofa. Her mother followed her. For a moment, she just stared at Vanessa. She placed her arm around her shoulders. "You know, I went to church today. I prayed for you. I asked God to make His presence known in your life. I asked him to ease your pain and to bring you joy, to put peace in your heart."

"I don't want peace, Mom. I want death."

She knew by the look of pain on Vanessa's face that she meant it. Her heart pounded against her chest, and her breath became shallow. Certainly, Vanessa wouldn't try to kill herself. The doctor assured her that people usually don't try to kill themselves after their first attempts. But that didn't ease the panic that rose inside her.

"I know you feel that you want to die, but you really don't. It's just the pain talking. You just need prayer. The day is going to come when what you're experiencing is going to be a distance memory, when you're going to have a life full of love," her mother said as she rocked Vanessa back and forth. "I know better than anyone what you've lost. Everything that was taken from you, God will give back to you. If you just hang in there, the reward at the end of this journey is going to be amazing. God is going to work it out for you; just wait on Him. God makes no mistakes, and He has a reason for everything that He does, whether we see it or not."

"Mom, don't," Vanessa said, pulling away from her mother's embrace.

"Don't what?"

"Don't give me your 'God is good' speech. I don't want to hear it," she said, exhausted. Vanessa started to pace the floor.

"Vanessa," Alice called tenderly.

"Mom, you have the faith. Good for you. You should be faithful and sing His praise. He hasn't taken anything from you."

Her mother jumped up and stood in front of Vanessa to prevent her from pacing.

"'Hasn't taken anything from me'? How can you say that? You are my child and I love you. When you hurt, I hurt, and so does anyone that loves you. Those were my grandbabies. I loved them very much. I was there for each of their births, and Joe was like a son to me."

"It's not the same, Mom."

"And I lost a child that day. I lost you, Vanessa. You haven't been the same since their deaths, and no one is blaming you. You've had a lot to deal with. You're in pain, and I get that, but you're not the only one in pain. So don't stand there and tell me I haven't lost anything. Everyone who loves you and your family has lost something. But your loss is unimaginable in comparison to ours. No matter how much we hurt, God can heal us if we allow Him. He's merciful, He's—"

"He's a joke, Mom," she said with laughter in her voice. "He's not merciful. If He's so merciful, why didn't He allow me to die with my family? Why would he condemn me to live the rest of my life alone? Where is the mercy in that? To rip a mother's children and the man she chose to spend her life with from her. Where is the mercy in that?"

"I don't have the answers, baby, and I don't know why He does what He does. I do know that it's not for us to question the will of God."

"The will of God? That's funny, Mom, I have a will too. I *will* not serve a God that will plague my life with so much sorrow and hardship. *That's* my will. I will not serve a God that has no mercy. How's that for His will, Mom? Let yourself out. I will not talk about this any longer."

"I'm not finish talking to you."

"If you're going to talk about the will of God, yes ma'am, you are," Vanessa said as she stood, taking a tissue from the box of Kleenex that was on the coffee table and wiping her eyes. She tied her robe closed and walked up the stairs.

Alice couldn't believe what she had just heard. A woman who had once loved God had nothing but contempt for him now. Picking up her purse, she glance at the TV. She instantly recognized the DVD that was playing. It was Vanessa and Joe's tenth wedding anniversary.

That explains it, Alice thought to herself. Vanessa was only reacting from the grief that the video brought on. She looked toward the stairs, making sure Vanessa had disappeared from view. She said a silent prayer for Vanessa then left, taking the DVD with her.

~Be sure to grab your copy of A Second Chance at Love by Pamela Wright in stores November 1st~

A Special Message from LaQueisha Malone to her Readers

Dear *Loyal Readers,*

Putting this book together wasn't that tough at all for me. *A Walk In My Shoes* is the re-release of my 2008 release, *A New Pair of Shoes Step In Mine.* I was not satisfied with the outcome of that release. It only contained 60 pages, which 48 of them were poetry. I felt my readers deserved more. I couldn't go on to completing my novels until I gave the very best I could in this book.

Unlike Cell of the Mind (2011), all the poems in this book were written during my teenage years. It is a glimpse of my life. As a teenager in high school, trying to make it through puberty, we all experience great emotions. Sometimes these emotions feels like the end of the world as we know it. For me, I wrote down those emotions and feelings. Putting them down on paper made me feel as though I shouted it out. I don't know if anyone has been through similar situations, but I know some teenage girl or boy will be able to relate.

I hope you have enjoyed this journey into my teenage years. These poems were written during some hard times for me, whether it was family, relationships, or spiritual.

I had so many dreams during those years, but fear of failing kept me secluded. It kept me thinking I could never be good enough as a writer. I would write and throw the pages away when finished. Someone read my writing one day, and bragged to me how they were able to relate to my words. It was then I realized I was not alone in my feelings, and I could help someone else.

Growing up, friendship wasn't something that came easy for me. I was quiet and very much a loner. I mostly wrote or daydreamed a lot. I observed a lot, and learned quickly how friends can turn enemy fast.

In this book, you will see a bit of my feelings with my parents' divorce. It was hard for me, because I wanted both parents in the home. I wanted my Daddy there throughout my young relationships. I wanted my Daddy there to talk to whenever I felt like it. Sharing him with another family, as a child, was hard.

As I got older, I began to seek spiritual guidance. At that point in my life everything began to make sense to me. I learned to trust in God. Through reading and studying His word, I learned if you apply it to your life, you can understand your purpose.

Thank you once again for reading.

I Appreciate You,

LaQueisha Malone

LAQUEISHA MALONE was born and raised in Arkansas, where she currently resides with her family. She has worked as a Psychiatric Aide at a children's Habilitation Center for 9 years, and is currently the Secretary of the Education Department at the same Habilitation Center.

Writing has always been a part of her life. She began writing fiction stories and poetry about the age of 13. It was her way of coping with everyday situations. She accredits Dr. Maya Angelou for her love of writing poetry.

Her poetry has been entered into numerous contests, and many of them were published in book and CD compilations through *The International Library of Poetry*. She also won many awards for these publications.

In 2013, LaQueisha Malone launched her own publishing company STRAWBERRY PUBLICATIONS. She wants to offer Authors a ripened experience of publishing. For more information visit www.strawberrypublications.com

She is currently promoting **Cell of the Mind** and **A Walk In My Shoes** while working on her next book.

Other Titles by La Queisha Malone

☐ *Cell of the Mind*
$12.95 x ___ = _____

☐ *Secrets Amongst Friends*
COMING SOON

☐ *Eyes of Her Mother*
COMING SOON

Order your autograph copies of these other great titles from LaQueisha Malone.

Print Name

_____

Mailing Address

_____

_____

Email _____

NOTE: Add $5.80 s&h for 1ˢᵗ item and $1.00 s&h per item thereafter. Make check or money order payable to '**LaQueisha Malone**'. Mail all correspondence to LaQueisha Malone; PO Box 895; Rison, AR 71665

Cell of the Mind = _____
Secrets Amongst Friends = _____
Eyes of Her Mother = _____

Total Amount Enclosed: $_____

Strawberry Publications Titles

www.strawberrypublications.com

www.ingramcontent.com/pod-product-compliance
Lightning Source LLC
Chambersburg PA
CBHW060800050426
42449CB00008B/1471